IRON
ROSE

A Pilot Press Book

ALSO BY ERIC GREINKE:

Sand & Other Poems
Caged Angels
The Last Ballet
Grape Wishes (With Ben Tibbs & Ronnie Lane)
10 Michigan Poets (As Editor)

IRON
ROSE

Poems By Eric Greinke

ISBN 0-88324-054-8
Bound in boards: $4.50

FIRST EDITION

ACKNOWLEDGMENTS

Certain of these works have previously appeared in the following publications: *AMARANTHUS; BITTERROOT; ESSENCE; GRAPE WISHES* (Limited Edition book with Ben Tibbs & Ronnie Lane. 1973, Pilot Press Books); *HAPPINESS HOLDING TANK; POSTCARD* (Joie Editions broadside. 1973); *HOT APPLES* (Anthology edited by Gay Rubin. 1973, Hot Apples Press); *KING JAMES VERSION; PEACE & PIECES ANTHOLOGY* (Edited by Maurice Custodio. 1973, Peace & Pieces Books); *UT REVIEW; THE WOODSRUNNER*. *"The Owls"* is a loose paraphrase of the first stanza of *"Les Hiboux"* by Charles Baudelaire. *"The Rendezvous"* was written in collaboration with my wife, Pamela. For any omissions from this list, my apologies.
                                    – *Eric Greinke*

Printed in the United States of America

Published by PILOT PRESS BOOKS,
P.O. Box 2662, Grand Rapids, Michigan   49501

Contents

This book is for Ben Tibbs

"Roses grow in a ribcage."

CROSSING

Crossing

We are moving   through the door.
These floors   sway with the tide
of the ejaculating train.   You lean
on me for support.   I am leaning on you
tonight   for support.   We grasp hands
& the hands open up & graft together.
The blood flows freely between us.   We are
swimming   spinning   through the door.

Crossing over   the frontier   we
hold our breaths   anticipating
the cold plunge.   I am your support
in my dependence.   You are crying.
Go ahead.   The rushing snow inside us
now   rushing   pushing   as outside the train
the country is white   with anticipation.

This is the entrance.   Go ahead through.
The grey clouded ceiling will protect us.
I can feel your blood   bubbling in confusion.
You are afraid to go ahead   afraid to
return.   Your fear   is my support.   I will
hold you inside me   behind me   as the
hard & emptied train   pulls away.

Iron Rose

(For Christine Zawadiwsky)

The petals are opened
in wrought-iron levels
& layers.   Black blood
is hard as a lover's hatred.
It freezes on the stem.

The wind
brought metal seeds
to grow here
on this cold stamen.

This pistol
shot black bullets
into the postal wind.
I knew its stones would find you,
transform you,   enter you.

The vast expanse,
a lake   a desert,
softens beneath
these seeds.

This rose has teeth.
It has hard leaves like
sterile dreams,   its seeds
like letters chuting through the wind,
through time   with old lines.

Like seeds   like dreams,
opened days later
in new hands   to wet new eyes,
new roses weld themselves

into your thighs.

The Spider

The web is light.
It screens down those
who fly too close.

> A gnat flew through.
> It missed the sticky threads
> on all sides.   It found
> a window in the deadly net.

*   *   *   *   *

I look out the window at the lighted day.

It is bordered on both sides

by course black curtains.

Hidden

I will curl like a mouse
in the hollow of a root
at the foot of a tree,
& you will not find me.

You'll come to me on wings
of little grey sparrows.
I'll be a white stallion,
& you will not catch me.

Roses

(For My Mother)

1.

Her body is a rosethorn
slashing through my flesh.

2.

I found a single rose
alone & freezing on the snow.

Still alive,
I held it in my hand
& watched it turn white.

3.

I went to slice a rose
from its stem;
like a spider suspended above a flame,
I held my razor poised.

My face felt hot,
but I did not cut.

4.

In the universe of the rose
I dance before a mind
higher than my own.

I hold it in my hand.
I touch its petals with my lips.
An electric charge
burns through my blood.

5.

There are white roses
all around the room,
& black horses
with red roses
in their long manes.

6.

Her body is black & open
on the white sheet.
Red petals of roses
are all around her.

I hold her in my hand
& watch her sleep.

7.

I've seen them climb
on their vines
up over fences.

I went up close
to hear their speech,
& could feel the heat
of their silence.

8.

She slices deeper into me.
When I see her in my sleep
she kisses me;
but when I try to touch her
she disappears.

9.

I've seen her dancing beneath the moon.
When she was done
she dove into the ground
& was gone.

10.

Roses in the morning
shiver in new light.
Transformation complete,
they relax until evening.

11.

I've seen her coming in before sunrise,
scratches on her thighs & breasts.

12.

Thorns cut the skin.
The skin opens &
thin women run out
on the palm of my hand.

Snow

1.

Sugar sifts into the cup.   Disappears
in brown coffee.   Hides a bitter taste.

Your face.   Your mouth.   Your brown skin.
My white hot seed hidden   within you.

2.

Snow burns the ground.
The sound you made when darkness
settled in   spread out   smothered us.
We were sleeping then.
We are sleeping now.

3.

I can see tracks
in the snow.
I'm going away,
but I don't know where.

5.

We've been sleeping.   Books on the shelves
are sleeping.   Shadows.   Bitter shapes.
Dreams of dead men.

6.

Snow burns into me.   Buries me.   Crazes
me.   Freezes me   into sleep.

I'm going away   but I don't know where.

Snow sifts into the brown landscape.
Your face.   My seed.   I'm going away.

I don't know where.

The Tree

Three trees stand at the top
of the hill.   Surrounded by
rocks & boulders.

Flowers.

The girl is young.
She stoops & breaks
a flower from its stem.

Later that night the stem wilts & falls.

The trees stand black against the whining wind.

The rocks below.   Snakes curl from the cracks.

Snakes wind around the stems of the flowers.

Hearts

(For Jeff, Joe, Rosie & Christine)

1.

The mainspring tightens.
The blood flows backwards.
The mirror fades blank.

The clock winds toward the last tick.

2.

I was almost dead when you
pressed your hearts to mine.

& now there are five faces
smiling in my mirror.

Thanks for the exchange.
Things are better here.

The Insomniac

I lay awake
where the river bends:
the jams of logs,
the broken, confused
rocks, (heads of frightened
bathers), deep funeral places.

I breathe in the murky shadows.
I float incessantly
above the weeds.   I suck
the black muck.   Every morning
I am killed by the hot passing sun.

The Owls

The owls are remote
in the black woods
like strange gods.

Their eyes blast fire.
They meditate.

The Poet In His Rose Garden

(For Peter & Dyann)

One day he was looking
for his unicorn,
& the Huntress pierced his heart
with her arrow,
& now he sends his friend
a photo of himself
in a rose garden.
He smiles,
book in hand,
surrounded by thorns & sweet petals.
He is not afraid of pain or joy.
They cannot hurt him.
Roses flow through his veins.

The photo could've been taken
a hundred years ago:
he looks like Whitman,
with bearded face & straw hat.
But he is from the British Isles,
& has lived with natives in Africa,
where poems still burn wild
from ancient jungle drums:
he has no time to worry about time:
roses do not grow in dry dust.

He seeks the language of the rose.
He has no time for common speech,
no time for dreams of tv scenes
or cars or yards or paneled streets:
he searches for his unicorn,
his soul's desire,
his Lady of the Unpolluted Lake.
This is no demented, Quixotic dance.
Roses grow in his ribcage,
& behind him in the photo
I can see
the holy, horned horse:
smiling back at me.

Seeds

(For Thomas Fitzsimmons)

"But friend!
            What will grow
      in this dust,
                without any water
      or wind?"

"Tiny seeds."
            he said.

                        &,

                        they did.

PAINTING

Painting

(For Roy Carruthers)

Lines. Twenty snowy mountains.
The eye of the blackbird.
Van Gogh at St. Remy. Screaming in sun colors.

Leaves ride the gutters
through the streets. In the shadows
lonely men pass. An owl screeches the wind

through the fingers of the trees.
The river is moving. Singing madly
through time.

Green

Angry trees move
through dark fields.
Dogs run
on moonlit hills.
Bats whine & dip
up & down.

Two green eyes
in this room.
The lips are red.
Shadows rock
on the edge
of the black ocean.

The trees gasp,
& twist.
The dogs howl
against the moon.
Two green lights
in this drowning room.

The Snowy Fields

(For Robert Bly)

1.

Driving through the new snow
between the silent fields.   Michigan.

If I was to walk across that field
I'd meet myself coming quietly back
through the snow.   A ghost.

2.

The whole country
is snowing today.
Everyone everywhere
is alone today.
Like the sparrows
that shiver on the wires.

Your House

(For Donald Hall)

The basking plants listen, breathe our conversation.
They thrill at one recognition, relax when smiles break
From bearded faces. They watch the secret cats slink
Lazy pathes along the Indian floors.

Soupbowls smile wide from the table. From the shelves
The books are sullen & uninterested in plans
To father them baby sisters. Photographs & prints glare
Through their glass, sometimes flash our faces back at us.

Tears

(For Ben Tibbs)

Crowds roll frozen eyes
toward the crazy foil of the moon

Insane chords of thunder splash
between the earth & the madly melting sun

Tall trees fall terrified
under the weight of the wild rain

& churchbells laugh
above the drunken clouds

Black

(For Duane Locke)

Vast black cats walk
the roofs of the dreaming houses.
Snowy ravens
with their wings spread wide & broken
are crucified
above the purple chapel door.
Negro doves sing
through the pale caucasian midnight.

I gave my love black roses
to wear in her bloodblack hair.

The Moon Is Red

There is blood
upon the road.

The river runs silently to the sea

She breathes hard,
her wind returning
from the night sky.
The hot feeling
remains: she can
still feel the throb
moving like a snake
deep inside her.

The snow falls helplessly to the earth

The night is cold
along the long road.

Through Revolving Time

(For Herbert Martin)

1.

birds
sing wild
in the ever-singing
sunlight
in the ever-turning
sky
sing high
through revolving time
like words
in the still
night

2.

birds
sing high
through revolving time
like words
sing wild
in the still
sunlight
in the ever-singing
sky
in the ever-turning
night

3.

like words
in the still
sky
in the ever-turning
sunlight
birds
sing wild
sing high
through revolving time
in the ever-singing
night

Soon

Shadows whisper
through the halls.
Moonlight licks
against the glass.
Below the window
on the snow
a bird's ghost
leaves its body
& rises toward the moon.
Someone crying now
in another room.

Something's going to happen,

soon.

Postcard

The sky is grey here.
My room is quiet & near.
Thinking of you
　　　　　in my little cocoon.

The Islands

The islands lift their heads
above the waves;
each a brief relief,
                    suspended.

Old Gold

(For Donald Hall)

1.

You say that age
is the sun's moving
down stone hills
to a yellow sky.

      I can see 2 blackbirds there:
      nailed & hanging in the whispering wind.

            Yellow passes into red
            & red bleeds back
            into black.

2.

You love the sun.
You hate the sun.
The moon reflects light
as an afterthought.

      I can see 2 haloed faces there:
      helpless & lost in colorless space.

            Red burns into black
            & black flashes back
            into white.

The Rendezvous

Although she thought better of it,
Betty bought a ticket for the
Country, where she knew
Don waited for her.
Eagerly, willfully, almost
Fanatically, checking the chamber of the
Gun in her purse, she
Hid it once again beneath the
Indigo gloves she always kept
Just next to the
Kangaroo-skin muff. She
Laughed to herself, as the train left
Minneapolis, Minnesota.
Next stop:
Oshkosh, Wisconsin. Children
Played up & down the
Quiet aisles, pacifiers keeping the
Roar down to a low level of combustion.
Suddenly, the train jerked to a halt,
Taking Betty by surprise & landing her
Under the seat of the man in front of her.
Vaguely annoyed, he
Withdrew the
Xerox copy he carried of the
Yankee CONSTITUTION, exclaiming: "Your
Zeal is hardly warranted, young woman!"

Carnage

(For Ronnie Lane)

The snake slides along the trail.
Stops.   Seems to listen.

                    No sound.

It slowly recoils
its head back, over its tail.
& then it

          swallows itself into
          a perfect vibrating circle.

Burning

(For Alan Britt)

1.

Leaving, you may go
to Pluto, or to
another island.

It's like when
you mark a coin,
& it returns to your hand.

You go to bed,
fall into a dream,
& wake up dead.

2.

Some form
flies past your
window.
Some form of
some thing
that used to be
some other
thing.

Your hand
feels your face
involuntarily.
You find
you are
somebody else.

3.

Getting there,
you find yourself
where you always were.

It's like seeing someone
you've never seen before,
but they seem familiar.

You eat an orange
& feel teeth
biting your flesh.

4.

It's like you fall asleep,
& wake to see
your own shadow
staring at you.

What To Do Next

You arrive at the station
with your pockets full of time.
You're so invisible
that girls walk right through you.
Throw away your ticket
& skate away.

The clouds burn out
& ashes rain upon your head.
Your bones ache
from being used as jail bars.
Get up & move on
to the next holdup.

A dog on the coffee table.
A roller-derby in the ice cream.
A piano roaring down the road.
A monkey with a gun
has got you covered.
Keep your eyes straight ahead.

She has too much
but she wants a little more.
The room is loud
& the walls are turning brown.
Your ears are burning with old sounds.
Don't die.

Just take a deep breath,
                    get up,
                            & fly.

Photo of Eric Greinke by his wife, Pamela.